# THE ADVENTURES OF FRANK AND ANDREW:
# The Mystery of the Stolen Gadgets

Pranav Mahesh

# DEDICATION

To my parents, who put up with me when I was using their laptop every day to write this novel

# TABLE OF CONTENTS

# ACKNOWLEDGMENTS

Thank you to all the people who helped me in writing this book:

My Mom and Dad, who let me write my novel, and who eagerly awaited for its publication.

The NaNoWriMo Website and Helpers, who sponsored the contest to write a novel.

My 6th grade teacher Ms. Kosh, who took the time to read and fix errors in my novel when she could have been helping other students instead.

# CHAPTER 1:
## FALLING OUT OF THE SKY

"Whee!" 12 year old Frank said, with a triumphant look glued to his face.

"HELP ME!" Frank's brother, Andrew said. He was also 12. Frank had dark black hair and was wearing a red shirt. Andrew had blond hair and was wearing a light blue shirt.

Frank was 4' 6" and Andrew was 4' 5", so Frank was a bit taller than Andrew, but not much. Frank's eyes were dark brown and Andrew's eyes were a gentle green. Frank was born on January 13, 2001, and Andrew was born on January 29, 2013.

"I have acrophobia, you know!" Andrew complained. "Why am I even related to you?"

"Because you're my brother, and I don't care that you have a fear of heights!" Frank answered.

"Save me!" Andrew pleaded.

"SSSHHH!" Frank said, with a frown. The wind was flapping in their face while gravity pulled them down towards the ground.

Frank and Andrew were falling from the sky when they jumped out of their private plane because they needed to visit an important place.

When Andrew asked Frank why they could not take their private plane down to the city, Frank said, "It's better to make a big entrance." Andrew shook his head in exaggerated agony. *Why me?* he thought.

You're probably thinking, *But what happens if their parachute fails?* Well, Frank had read the Encyclopedia Brown series, and in one of the stories he said that a skydiver was supposed to have 2 parachutes, in case one failed. Frank told Andrew, and here they are!

Andrew closed his eyes.

"Tell me when we're there!!" he yelled.

*Okay, maybe I'm acting a little bit too scared,* Andrew thought.

He liked the sensation, but he did not want Frank to notice. He just tried to enjoy the moment while it lasted, so he spread his arms out and relaxed.

30 seconds later, (Andrew counted) Frank yelled, "Hello! Earth to Andrew! Open your parachute – now!" He already had his parachute open.  Andrew opened his eyes. They were dangerously close to the city. Andrew pulled the cord that triggered the mechanism inside his backpack. His chute opened.

"Brothers," he muttered as they drifted down slowly and gracefully.

"Cheer up!" Frank said to Andrew. "We're finally at Las Vegas, Nevada!" And indeed they were! There was the Mandalay Bay which was a resort which was at their left, with bright sea green water and a sandy beach. Palm trees surrounded the area.

Building of various sizes, and colors were planted on the ground. The Stratosphere Tower, which was 1,149 feet, was the biggest building in Las Vegas. Luckily, when Frank and Andrew landed, they were above a field next to a farm, and not a bottomless abyss.

"FRANK! ANDREW! FRANK! ANDREW!" the people from the city chanted.

"Hey, how come they say your name first?" Andrew asked.

"Because it has a better ring to it." Frank shot back at Andrew. And secretly, Andrew had to agree. Frank had one syllable and Andrew had two syllables. It made it sound better if they said Frank's name first, right? No, wait it - What? You do not get it? Well, what I'm trying to say here is – oh, never mind. You wouldn't get it anyway.

"Luckily, the people that are watching are far away, so when we land, we won't be chased all over town." Andrew said.

"That's probably the first witty thing that you said in your life!" Frank said. Andrew rolled his eyes.

"Uh-huh. Really." he said in a monotone voice and a deadpan expression. "Well, I do have my moments."


"Hey look, it's Frank and Andrew!" Frank and Andrew saw some little girls staring at them wearing shirts that said, 'I ♥ FRANK AND ANDREW'.

"We're on the way to stardom!" Andrew told Frank,

bumping his shoulder.

"In the wondrous world of Frank, that's not really funny."

"Now, girls, let's do our thing!" the leader said.

"AAAHHHH!!!" they screamed in delight in a high-pitched voice as they chased Frank and Andrew.

"AAAHHHH!!" Frank and Andrew screamed, not in delight. They ran and ran. Finally, they dived into a small green bush.

"Where are they?" they inquired.

"Quick, put on your black jacket and let's put on our fake mustaches and beards! Fast!" Frank hissed.

"Let's put on the Mind Communicators, too!" Andrew said. Now they had the ability to read each other's minds. The hats established a 10 feet connection to the nearest Mind Communicator.

They also put on hats over their Mind Communicators, so that the girls did not know they had a gadget on their heads. Frank and Andrew peeked out from the bush.

"Come on, move forward, move forward," Frank whispered.

As if by magic, the girls moved forward.

Frank and Andrew snuck up behind them. They whistled innocently as they went in the opposite direction. The girls jumped and said, "Who are you guys?" Frank and Andrew exchanged nervous glances.

*We didn't think about that,* Frank's voice spoke Andrew's mind.

*Allow me,* Andrew thought, as he stepped up and said, "Hi, my name is umm... Jack and this is uh... Bernice!"

Frank stepped on Andrew's foot and shot him his ultimate patented threatening glare, deployed at maximum power, and if looks could kill, well, we could just say that Andrew wouldn't be here right now.

Andrew gulped.

The leader scrutinized them. "You look familiar, but I just can't place the face."

Andrew thought in his mind, *Please don't say it's us.*

"Oh, well, it doesn't matter."

Frank and Andrew almost let out a sigh of relief if they hadn't caught themselves at the right time.

"Jack and Bernice, have you seen Frank and Andrew?" the girls inquired, tapping their feet impatiently.

"You mean Frank and Andrew, the famous detectives? They're here?! Yikes, we have got to find them! MUST! GET! AUTOGRAPH!" Andrew said with his big, fat, wide, not-quite-fibbing eyes. The girls sighed and walked away, and Frank and Andrew took off.

# CHAPTER 2:
## SOMETHING IS DEFINITELY FISHY

P *hew,* Frank said in his mind.

*Too close,* Andrew added.

Now, you're probably thinking:

*Wait. Frank and Andrew are famous detectives?*

Well, that's not all. They are secret agents, who are part of the E.S.A.F. or as agents call it, the Elite Secret Agency Force. Non-agents called it the Everyday Shopping Apple Facility. People actually believed it, which just shows how ignorant they were. And yes, it was disguised as a Shopping Center.

And this was why they were being parachuted into Las Vegas in the first place. There was a sign on the windowsill that said "OUT OF BUSINESS" because they were not "earning enough money," so people wouldn't go in. Andrew made sure no one was watching, and Frank put the key inside the slot. They heard a click, and the honks of cars whizzing past them, so they dove inside the building.

"I never knew you were such a good liar. I mean, come

on. Jack is okay, but Bernice?! That has got to be the most absurd and ridiculous name that I've heard." Frank said to Andrew.

"Hey, don't say that. I was under pressure. Plus, there are probably people out there named Bernice." Andrew responded.

"Fine." Frank said, with a glum face. "I'm sorry, whoever's out there with the name Bernice."

Andrew smiled. *Victory*, he thought.


The E.S.A.F was still disguised as a shopping center. Frank pushed the red secret button hidden beneath the apple stand. The windows closed so no one could see.

"Please enter the password. If you do not know what you are doing, please exit immediately. Press one for help." A robotic voice said. Andrew jumped. "Huh? What was that? Oh, you pushed the button." He said. Frank entered his passcode. He punched in the numbers 8-4-5-2 and clicked Enter.

"Match! Please further verify by using the hand scanner." Frank put his hand on the hand checker. The voice said, "Frank – Agent 8452 - Access Granted!"

Andrew tried to enter his passcode, 5-4-1-6. He entered 5-4-1-7. "Match!" the voice said. He put his hand on the hand checker.

"INVALID HAND!" the voice warned. "RED ALERT! CODE 404!" Alarms began to bleep and blare. Lasers came out and began to surround Frank and Andrew.

"Attention!" a voice like a fire truck said. "You have 30

seconds before spontaneous combustion!"

"You idiot," Frank sighed. "Luckily, I read the manual."

He pushed in his passcode in reverse, 2-5-4-8 and matched his hand. The lasers stopped charging. Andrew entered his passcode, 5-4-1-6 and matched his hand. The alarms stopped beeping and blaring.

The robotic voice said, "Match! Andrew – Agent 5416 – Access Granted!"

The door opened.

"Come in!" a calm voice soothed.

Frank and Andrew went inside the door. It was a big room. There were gadgets on a shelf on the left. There was a soda dispenser on the right. A big TV stood in the middle, saying E.S.A.F. in golden letters. In tiny font below the logo, it said Elite Secret Agency Force. Andrew was nervous. He tugged on the collar of his shirt, and he made a cringing sound. Frank rolled his eyes.

"Hi, chief." they both said. The chief swiveled around in his chair to face the boys. He was wearing a black jacket with a real mustache. His hair was slicked back so he would look cool. His smile looked flawless, and his eyes were electric blue.

He was wearing black Super-Spy glasses, just one of the other gadgets the E.S.A.F. uses. They had night vision, X-Ray vision (Yuck!), and laser eyes that could pierce through metal. The glasses were only reserved for high-rank agents. Frank and Andrew were not high-rank agents, yet. Little did they know their life was about to change...

"Hello, boys." the chief said. He was eating kettle popcorn.

"Um… chief, you look different." Andrew said. Frank elbowed him.

"Ouch!" Andrew said, rubbing his stomach.

"Oh, um…" the chief said nervously. Then his eyes lit up. "I went to the spa and had some people give me a makeover! You know, so our enemies wouldn't recognize me!"

"That's clever," said Andrew with a happy face. Frank rubbed his chin thoughtfully. Something was not right here.

"Anyway, I have some important footage for you. Would you care to watch it?" he asked, eager to change the subject.

Frank and Andrew shrugged.

"I'll take that as a yes," he said and turned the TV on. "Lights!" he called and the lights went out. They looked at the image starting to form on the 52 inch TV.

"Darn these wires," the chief said as he struggled to plug them in to make the TV screen clearer.

"Come on… getting clearer… clearer… clearer… There!" Andrew said. The chief took some popcorn and put it in his mouth. At first the image was hard to see, but it got clearer and they realized it was when Andrew entered the wrong passcode.

"Attention! You have 30 seconds before spontaneous combustion!" a fire truck like voice said. Lasers pointed at them.

"Bwah-haha!!" the chief burst out laughing. Popcorn flew out of his mouth, nearly hitting both of them. Frank rolled his eyes.

"If laughing was hazardous to your health, then you'd be in intensive care right now." he said.

"Ahhh..." Andrew said, wiping a fake tear from his eye. "I remember it like it was 5 minutes ago..."

"IT WAS 5 MINUTES AGO!" Frank shouted.

"Jeez, temper, temper." Andrew said with a smug look. Frank looked like he was ready to kill anything in sight.

"Since you boys proved you can handle yourselves in an emergency, you are promoted to be high-rank agents and you get the Super-Spy glasses!" the chief yelled in excitement.

"WHOO-HOO!!" they both shouted. The chief pressed a button and streamers fell to the ground. They partied until it was night. (Okay, it didn't happen, but it can't hurt to dream, can it?)

"Alright, here are your spy glasses!" the chief said as he handed them to Frank and Andrew.

"Cool!" Andrew exclaimed. They put them on and they fit snug like a glove. They looked like 3-D glasses with one lens red and another lens red. They had buttons on the side and Andrew fooled around with it. "What does this button do?" He pressed it. Beep! Beep! Data swirled around inside.

"Whoa..." Andrew said. He pointed it at the chief. "Wait, what? His power level is OVER 9000?!"


"Nobody says that anymore," Frank said.

"But it is!" Andrew said, protesting.

No one bought it. Crickets seemed to chirp.

"Alright, now I want you to read the manual." the chief said, with a sly grin.

"Manual, shmanual. What does this button do? Is this night vision? AWESOME!" Andrew exclaimed.

"NO! HEY!" the chief said.

*Bzzztt!*

Lasers shot out of the glasses, nearly frying a nearby gadget.

"Oops..." Andrew said with a sheepish look on his face.

"Oops? OOPS?! WHAT is that supposed to mean?" Frank said angrily.

"Um...uh..." Andrew muttered.

While this was all happening, the chief had turned around. Before the boys knew, he turned around and as fast as lightning, threw the heavy book at the boys.

"Yikes!" Frank yelled. He got out of the way in time, but Andrew wasn't so lucky.

WHAM!

The book hit him on the head and he fell to the ground.

"Andrew! Speak to me! Are you okay?" Frank yelled with worry.

"Not... okay..." Andrew murmured. His eyelids were closing and he blacked out.

# CHAPTER 3:
## MORT "EVIL" CLAYTON

Frank kept shouting his name, but Andrew didn't respond. His eyelids remained shut.

"HEY!" he yelled to the chief. "Why did you do that to him?!"

"Oh, that's simple," the chief said. "Because I want to kill you!" He pressed a button on his belt and transformed. He didn't change shape. He didn't become a monster. It seemed like he was changing his features, his hair color, and his eye color. It looked like he was becoming another person! His hair color was blacker and his eyes were not comforting. They were black and harsh. His Super-Spy glasses flew into his pocket.

"At last, I can get out of that hot costume! Man, it was sizzling in there!" the "chief" said. His voice was not soothing. It was angry, loud, and deep.

"Who are you?!" Frank yelled.

"I am Mort Clayton!" he yelled.

"What does that mean?" Frank inquired.

"Mort means death. And Clayton means..." he

hesitated to say it.

"Isn't Clayton the evil guy in Tarzan?" Frank asked.

"Arrgh! I hate it when people say that!" he yelled.

"But it's true," Frank said, smiling.

"Never mind that!" he growled. He gritted his teeth. "Evil is my middle name, and that proves what I'm going to do!"

Frank rolled his eyes. "Everyone says that."

"No, really, my full name is Mort Evil Clayton." he said.

Frank raised his eyebrows. "Didn't see that coming." he said.

"Stop making fun of my name!" Mort yelled. "I will steal all of your gadgets! Then we'll see who is laughing! I knew the other boy would not bother reading the manual."

"Why are you telling me your plan?" Frank asked.

"Because I know you can't stop me," said Mort with an evil grin.

"Oh, really," said Frank with a triumphant smirk. "What makes you think that I won't come to stop you?"

"Because of this!" Mort yelled. He pressed another button on his belt and a giant magnet burst out of his belt. "Behold my GADGET MAGNET!"

"Yikes!" yelled Frank.


The magnet sucked all of the gadgets into a large vacuum cleaner. Frank and Andrew's Super-spy glasses flew off their faces and into the vacuum cleaner. The bag got larger, and larger, and... larger. Gadgets began to fly off the walls. A laser, and a three in one gadget that had a pencil, pen, and stylus flew off. Frank held on to a shelf for dear life. His eyes were wide with shock and fear. His legs were wiggling towards the vacuum cleaner.

"Mwa-ha-ha!" Mort chortled.

The bag got larger until it was gigantic, and all the gadgets were sucked inside. The force of the vacuum cleaner stopped. Frank fell to the floor.

"I'll be on my way now!" he yelled.

He took out a gadget, the Teleportalight 5000, and pressed the button. He began to glow with an intensive yellow light. Frank looked away and when he looked again, he was gone.

"Darn it!" Frank yelled.

Frank's voice bounced off the walls. Everything seemed to be bare, and everything was still, quiet, and -

"M-M! M-M!"

Frank heard a struggling voice. He followed the sound. It was coming from the closet! Frank slowly tiptoed to the closet, and opened the door! He jerked back in case it was another bad guy trying to blast him. But it was not a bad guy. In fact, it was the opposite.


It was the real chief! He was tied and gagged!

"M-M-M!!" he said, his mouth muffled by rags.

*What? How – oh, here we go again,* thought Frank.

Frank ripped the duct tape off his mouth. RIP!

"YEOW!" the chief yelled.

Frank untied the rags tying the chief's arms. He rubbed his mouth. "What's going on?" he yelled. "I was working as usual, and then SOMEONE tied me up and threw me into the closet!"

"It was Mort Clayton!" Frank said with a worried expression.

"M-Mort... CLAYTON?! Oh, boy. Oh, no. Here we go again..." The chief shook his head and squeezed his head.

"He stole all the gadgets and knocked out Andrew!"

"WHAT?!" the chief yelled in anger.

"You know him, chief?" Frank asked.

A sad look crossed his face. "He... he used to be my... my best friend." he stuttered.

"WHAT?" Frank yelled.

"Yeah. He used to go to my school, Hills Pine Magnet Middle School. We were in 8th grade. We were really great friends at the time." Frank's eyebrows arched upwards.

"As I was saying, we were best friends. But all that ended, when I became popular. I invented a gadget for one of my fellow friends. I remember, we were 13 at the time. The gadget was..." The chief stroked his chin, as if he was trying to remember. "It was called the Thingamajigger. Or was it called the Jiggamawisser? Hmmm..." He stroked his chin again. Frank was listening intently as though he was a kindergartener during story time.

"Oh, well, it doesn't matter anyway. After that,

everyone began cheering for me, and I became popular. Then, Mort changed his attitude from a confident, jubilant kid, to a scary kid, in a dark corner. One day, he disappeared. And now he's back..." The chief's eyebrows furrowed. Frank stared at him with worry.

"He stole every single one of our gadgets!" Frank said.

The chief sighed. "I should have known this was going to happen. But luckily, I have a solution. Why don't you wake up your brother first?"

Frank went over to Andrew, who was still lying on the ground.

"ANDREW! ANDREW! WAKE UP!"

No response.

"ANDREW!! HEY!!"

No response.

Frank shook his head.

"Okay, let's use another alternative." the chief said, with a smile. He poured a glass of cold water into a bucket. Then, he put some ice cubes inside. Frank couldn't help but laugh. They held it together.

"Ready," the chief said. "Three! Two! One! GO!" They both dumped the ice cold water on Andrew.

"AAAHH!" Andrew screamed. He got up fast. "What was that for?" he asked. He was sopping wet and water began to drip from his shirt.

"Sorry, but you wouldn't wake up!" Frank said.

"Wait, where's the other chief?" he asked. The real

chief and Frank exchanged glances.

Frank said, "I'll explain it."

"Alright, so, what's going on here?" Andrew asked.

Frank began. "See, the last thing you remembered was the chief smashing the book on you, right?" Andrew nodded. "Well, after that, he transformed and changed into a different man!"

Andrew's eyes widened. So did the chief's. Although he had the quick version, he waited for Frank to tell him the full, action-packed story. "He said his name was Mort "Evil" Clayton."

Andrew frowned. "Isn't Clayton the evil guy in Tarzan?" he asked.

"Yeah, I said the same thing, but then he got angry," Frank explained. "And then, he got this giant magnet thing, and it sucked all the gadgets into a giant vacuum cleaner. And then he left. I heard some sounds from the closet door. I followed the sound, and the real chief was there, and he was gagged. And then, we decided to wake you up."

"Grrr... that fellow knocked me out!" Andrew yelled.

"Look on the bright side," Frank said. "At least you didn't get amnesia." Andrew glared at him.

"But how do we stand a chance now?" Frank asked. "He took all of our gadgets."

"I know," the chief said. "And that's why I have this." He pulled out a secret phone from his pocket and placed it in a socket on the wall. He pressed the buttons 03-09-19-58.

"That's my birthday," the chief explained. The wall

opened, and Frank and Andrew were dumbstruck.

# CHAPTER 4:
## GADGET STORAGE?!

There were tons of gadgets! There was one for every gadget that Mort stole. A sign on the top said, "EMERCY GADGET STORAGE – USE ONLY FOR EMERGENCIES!"

"Wait, what?!" Andrew asked in bewilderment.

"Huh?!" Frank asked. They gaped at the chief. "You never showed us that there was an emergency gadget storage!"

"Oops. Whatever!" the chief said. "Well, here are your new Super-Spy glasses."

"Yeah!" Andrew exclaimed, putting them on.

"And, for Andrew..." the chief handed Andrew a battery-powered hairdryer.

"Yeah!" Andrew exclaimed for the second time, turning the dryer on.

Frank smiled. "Let's hope Mort doesn't do that again."

"He won't," the chief said. "That bag might explode if it sucks too many gadgets inside, plus he doesn't know about this. He's not the only one that has secrets." Frank and Andrew sat down blue plastic chairs. The chief sat in his big swiveling chair.

"Oh, how I missed my swiveling chair." he said.

Frank and Andrew rolled their eyes.

"Whatever you say," Andrew said, trying to compress a smile.

"Hey!" the chief said. "I happen to like my chair!"

"Okay, okay, we're not here to discuss the chair." Frank said.

"Alright, back to the mission." the chief said. "Your goal is to find Mort, without any distractions. Capture him, and then bring back all the gadgets. You'll also need a disguise." The chief handed them a disguise. They were fancy clothes, as if they were going to a fancy restaurant. They both had a monocle to put on their eye. Both of them put their disguises on. Andrew put on a sophisticated look.

"Alright! We're back in business!" Andrew said, pumping his fist into his hand, very unsophisticatedly.

"His hideout is in a place called D.O.O.M. The address is 250 Fremont Street. It takes a few minutes to walk there. It's 6:00. If you're tired, go to a hotel first. Once you reach there, press the red button on the top left corner. Here are the keys to D.O.O.M. You'll also need some cash."

The chief handed them a key and $500. He threw random gadgets from the gadget storage into Frank and Andrew's backpacks.

"Alright, now get out! No dilly-dallying!" the chief said.

The boys put their glasses in their pockets, and then they went down in the elevator. Loud heavy metal music blasted in their ears.

"AAAHH!!" they screamed, holding their ears. Frank turned the volume down, and changed the station to smooth jazz. Andrew changed the station to action music. Frank changed it back to smooth jazz. Andrew changed it again to action music. They glared at each other. It was like watching a Ping-Pong game. They went back and forth, back and forth.

"Jazz!" Frank said.

"Action music!" Andrew said.

"JAZZ!"

"ACTION MUSIC!"

DING!

They had arrived at the first floor of the E.S.A.F. Frank and Andrew frowned at each other, shook their head, took a deep breath, and went outside. Then they both yawned.

"I'm tired," Frank said.

"Me too! Let's stay at a hotel." Andrew shook his head. "No, I mean, I fancy a cup of tea and some repose." Andrew said with an accent, adjusting his bowtie and monocle. Frank didn't know how Andrew had such a big vocabulary.

Andrew smirked at Frank. "You're not the only who uses big words," he said.

"Whatever." said Frank with a deadpan expression.

Andrew smiled triumphantly. *Victory... again,* he

thought.

It was evening, and the sunset was beautiful. The sky was a mix of orange and yellow. But it was ruined by the blinking lights of skyscrapers, company buildings like Pepsi, and the rush and honks of cars.

"Really is a busy day," Frank said.

They walked and walked. At last, they found a hotel. The banner said, "Las Vegas Supersize Hotel – Where all your needs are fulfilled."

"Looks nice," Andrew said. They walked in. There were tons of doors everywhere listed in alphabetical order. They said:

- Bathroom
- Cafeteria
- Elevator
- Game Room
- Golf Course
- Pool

"Wow..." Frank said.

The whole building was huge. A desk was on the left, and there . There was a huge chandelier above them. It was beautiful.

"We'd like to book a room," Andrew said, putting his hand on the desk.

"And there are two of you?" the clerk asked calmly.

"Yup," Andrew answered.

"That will be $150." the clerk said. Frank gave him $200. The clerk handed him back a $50 bill. "Okay, here is your room key. Your room is on the 5th floor." The clerk gave them a key that said 512 on it. "Please enjoy your stay at the Las Vegas Supersize Hotel."

Frank and Andrew walked to the elevator. Frank pushed the button.

DING!

The elevator opened. It had a green mat, and jazz music was playing inside. They walked in. Andrew pressed the button that said 5 and they went up.

"What, no remarks about jazz, now?" Frank asked.

"I've come to appreciate it. Can you think of a better place?" Andrew said.

Frank pretended to think about it. "Oh yeah! Home." he said.

DING!

They were at the 5th floor. They walked until they saw the room with the number 512 on it. Frank put the key and turned it, and the door clicked open. Andrew opened it.

"Wow..." Andrew said.

"Amazing!" Frank said.

# CHAPTER 5:
## NOW, THAT'S WHAT I CALL ENTERTAINMENT!

Their room was huge, and it had a 52 inch TV, a nice sofa with flower designs, two master bedrooms, and much, much more. There was even a big chandelier above them like the one they saw on the front lobby.

"Now that's what I call entertainment!" Andrew said.

"Mm-hmm..." said Frank, staring at the huge chandelier.

"HEY!" Andrew said.

Frank's vision cleared. He shook his head. "What?"

"You just were staring at the room, in a trance."

"I WAS NOT!"

"Yeah, you were."

"I DID NOT!"

"Yeah, right."

Frank's face turned red.

"You're blushing," Andrew remarked.

"Am not..." Frank muttered.

Andrew decided it was good to change the subject before Frank tried to hurt him. "Okay, so, I'll take one bedroom, and you'll take the other. Okay?"

"Yeah, couldn't hurt." said Frank.

"Before that, let's hit the game room!" said Andrew.

"Yeah!" said Frank.

They went inside the elevator and clicked 1st Floor. They went down. Ding! They had arrived at the first floor. They went into the door marked GAME ROOM.

"Wow... I have to admit, this place gets better and better." Andrew said. He snapped his fingers in front of Frank.

"What was that for?" Frank asked.

"Oh, just making sure you didn't fall into a trance again." Andrew laughed. Frank shot him his ultimate threatening glare deployed at maximum force, AGAIN. Andrew lowered his head.

The game room had a pool, an air hockey table, a ping pong table, a ball pit full of mini balls colored red, blue, yellow, and green, a huge slide that led into a soft fluffy carpet, and a huge waterslide that led into the pool. The pool was sea green, and was crystal clear.

Moments like this began to give a sense of peace to Frank. It looked just like a resort. He wanted to stay there... forever...

Frank closed his eyes, and breathed deeply. He just wanted to lie down, but Andrew just had to ruin his moment of peace. He dove into the ball pit, lied down on his back, and began to sink.

"Help! I'm sinking!" he said before he got buried by the balls. Frank dove inside the ball pit to save Andrew. Andrew, laughing, climbed up onto the platform that was above the ball pit.

"I can't believe you fell for that," he remarked.

Frank shot Andrew a glare.

"Oh, come on, lighten up." Andrew said.

Frank shot another glare at him.

"What's with this glare business?"

Another glare got shot from Frank.

Andrew shot Frank a glare this time.

Frank shot Andrew a glare.

As you can see, they probably would continue doing this, so let's fast forward to a minute later.

*One minute later...*

"Okay, I give up," said Andrew. Frank smiled.

"I'm going to go swimming. Do whatever you want." he said.

"I'll be inside our room." Andrew said.

"Okay, stay out of trouble."

"You sound like our mom back in Washington."

"Just stay out of trouble!" Frank gave Andrew the key.

"Alright, jeez!" Andrew said.

He exited the game room, went to the elevator, and he pressed the up button. The elevator came down to the first floor. Andrew stepped in and clicked on 5th floor.

He went upstairs to the 5th floor and walked down the row until he saw 512. He put the key in. The door clicked open. He sat on the sofa and saw a journal.

It said Frank's Journal – DO NOT OPEN! HEY, I'M TALKING TO YOU! Andrew got a screwdriver. Frank's journal had to have some alarm. He wouldn't leave it unguarded. Andrew carefully approached the journal, and opened it slowly. He was right. Alarms beeped and blared. Quickly, Andrew opened the circuits and disconnected them. He had a knack for rewiring circuit boards. He began to read at the first entry.

# CHAPTER 6:
## FRANK'S JOURNAL

*T*hursday, November 14

*Well, I'm Frank, and I'm 12. A month ago, I got a letter saying that I was qualified for a spot at the E.S.A.F., which they said was the Elite Secret Agent Force. Andrew, my brother, is also 12. He got a letter too. He just seems so... obtuse! That's the word.*

"Obtuse?" Andrew said, twitching his eye.

*He pretends to be a joker, but that could get him killed! As long as he listens to me, he wins in a fight. He needs to be a little more serious, like me.*

"Yeah, that'll happen," chuckled Andrew.

*Well, today, we skydived and made a big entrance. We are in Las Vegas, Nevada, where the secret quarters of the E.S.A.F. are. The chief sent us a notice saying that he wanted us to visit him and to train. Strangely, his handwriting was different than the time he sent the invitation. It didn't matter to us at the time.*

"Yeah, sure." Andrew said.

*Andrew was screaming. He's afraid of heights. He used the scientific word for fear of heights, acrophobia. I was hoping he wouldn't so I could say, "You have acrophobia?" and he would say, "What?" and I would say, "Excuse me; I keep forgetting how miniscule your vocabulary is."*

"But you couldn't," said Andrew.

*But I couldn't. Oh, well. What are you going to do?*

Andrew rolled his eyes.

*Then a bunch of girls wearing I ♥ FRANK AND ANDREW shirts came and chased us. We ran and ran and then we dived into a bush. Then, we put on our Mind Communicators and a disguise. Andrew came up with two names, Jack and Bernice. Personally, I think those are terrible names -*

"Hey, at least I had an idea!" said Andrew

*- but at least he had an idea. After that, they left us alone. Then, we went into the E.S.A.F. I verified my passcode and hand, and Andrew had to type in his passcode wrong...*

"Hey! It was an accident!" said Andrew.

*Alarms bleeped and blared and lasers pointed at us. But, luckily, I read the manual. You had to type your passcode in reverse, so I did. And then Andrew verified his hand and entered his passcode right.*

"That's when everything went wrong," remarked Andrew.

*That's when our life was turned upside down and everything went wrong.*

"I still wonder how Frank wrote this without me noticing," said Andrew.

*Oh, by the way, do you want to know how I wrote this without Andrew noticing? I simply asked the chief to make a gadget. He's good at making gadgets. He made a little bug thing that I keep in my hair. It connects through my mind to my journal, and whenever I think about my journal and what I've done, it gets downloaded into the journal. It's pretty ingenious...*

"Wow." Andrew said in awe.

*But, I always keep my journal in my pocket. This will be worth millions later on. Andrew won't have one. Ha! Okay, maybe I shouldn't laugh.*

*Where did I leave off? Oh yeah, well we went inside the door to the chief's office. Andrew was tugging on his collar and sweating. I had to stifle a laugh. And the first thing Andrew said to the chief was, "You look different."*

*I had to elbow him.*

"But he did look different!" exclaimed Andrew.

*But he did look strange. The chief said that he was given a makeover so that his enemies wouldn't recognize him. Andrew bought it, as usual. He doesn't think things through first.*

"Yeah, I do!" yelled Andrew.

*But, something definitely was not right the moment I scanned the chief. He was stuttering, and looked nervous. But he anxiously changed the subject. We watched a flashback of when Andrew entered the wrong passcode, and the chief burst out laughing, nearly spitting popcorn out of his mouth. Something was fishy. The chief never laughed that way.*

"Now that I think about it, that's right!" said Andrew.

*The chief told us that we were high-rank agents now. He gave us the Super-Spy glasses, which was only accessible to high-rank agents, and they have night vision, X-ray vision (I don't know why), lasers, etc.*

*The chief told us we had to read the manual. As usual, Andrew didn't read it –*

"As usual?!" Andrew said, flabbergasted.

*- And he fired a laser, thinking that it was night vision. He almost fried a nearby gadget. He really needs to be more serious. He really needs to read a manual. He shouldn't act like a joker. While I was busy yelling at him, the chief burst out with incredible reflexes and threw the book at us. I dodged out of the way, but Andrew didn't. The book hit him in the head and he fainted.*

"You could have saved me," remarked Andrew.

*Then I yelled at the chief and he pressed a button on his belt. Now I'm starting to hate buttons. You never know what's going to happen. Then he changed into a new person. He said his name was Mort "Evil" Clayton.*

*I teased him about his last name, and then he sucked all the gadgets, and this giant vacuum cleaner, and no gadgets, and... I'm not making much sense am I?*

"Not really," said Andrew.

*Well, he took the gadgets and that's when I found the chief tied and gagged. I removed the clothes tying his hand and ripped the duct tape off his mouth.*

"That's got to hurt," said Andrew, grinning.

*It must have hurt.*

*I told the real chief about Mort and his eyes bugged out. He told me that Mort used to be his best friend in school.*

"What?!" said Andrew, bamboozled, flabbergasted, and just plain confused.

*Oh, the irony. Well, they kind of separated their friendship when the chief became popular by inventing a gadget for one of the more popular kids. He called it the Thingamajigger. Or was it the Jiggamawisser?*

"Weird names," Andrew said.

*Well, one day, Mort disappeared. And now he's back. After the chief told me the story, we tried to wake up Andrew but it wouldn't work. So we dumped ice cold water on him. That woke him instantly.*

Andrew frowned.

*After explaining the story to Andrew, the chief gave us some money and since we were tired, we stayed at the Las Vegas Supersize Hotel. It was amazing! By the way, the chief gave us the key to Mort's evil headquarters called D.O.O.M.. Kind of fitting, don't you think?*

"No kidding," said Andrew.

*We got room 512. Andrew pretended to drown and the ball pit in the game room. He was laughing, so I shot my patented laser death glare, deployed at maximum force. That shut him up. It always works.*

"You think you're so awesome." Andrew said.

*All of my thoughts are stored inside this journal. I can't imagine what would happen if he got a hold on it.*

Andrew grinned evilly.

*But of course, that won't happen, unless he disconnects the alarm tied to this journal. But, I don't think he knows how to.*

"Oh really?" said Andrew with another devilish grin.

*Well, I'm taking a swim now. I have to take off the device in my hair or else it will malfunction. I wonder what Andrew is doing right now, upstairs. Well, see you later!*

# CHAPTER 7:
## LET'S LEAVE

C ool, I want one of these! I'm going to ask the chief for one. Andrew thought.

KNOCK! KNOCK!

"Uh, who is it?" Andrew asked.

"It's me, Frank!"

Uh oh, did an hour pass that fast? I better connect the alarms back. Oh dear, oh dear! Andrew thought.

"Coming, I'm in the bathroom!" he said.

"Ok!" Frank said.

Andrew quickly got to work and reconnected the alarms. In one minute it was done. Andrew kept the journal in the same spot where it was before and he opened the door. Frank came in and took a bath while Andrew relaxed listening to jazz.

"Oh, you're listening to jazz, huh?" Frank said as he came out from the shower with new clothes on.

"Can you stop that? I like jazz!" Andrew said.

Frank held his hands up in defeat. "Okay, if you say so."

It was 8:30, so they had an hour before they went to sleep.

They went downstairs.

Suddenly, Andrew had an idea. "You take the elevator, and I'll take the stairs." he said.

Frank looked at him strangely. "Why?" he asked.

"Just do it!"

Frank rolled his eyes, but he took the elevator, while Andrew jumped down each flight screaming, "Whee!"

He leaped like a kangaroo in a frog position so he could get more air. This was like skydiving, except it was way more fun.

Jumping, springing, and bouncing, Andrew pretended that he needed to dodge people running down the stairs.

Frank was downstairs, waiting for Andrew. He made a horrified face as Andrew leaped at him.

WHACK!

Frank flew backwards into the wall from the force of Andrew's leap. He slowly got up, dusted off his clothes, and glared at Andrew.

Andrew turned the other way, and whistled nonchalantly.

Frank took out his Super-Spy glasses and blasted Andrew with a low power laser. The impact didn't hurt Andrew, but it sent him flying backwards into the wall.

Andrew glared at Frank. Now everybody was looking at both Frank and Andrew strangely.

Frank and Andrew looked at each other, making a sheepish look. They both went to the elevator, and stepped inside.

"Sorry about that." Andrew said.

"Yeah, I'm sorry too. We should get some rest now. We leave in the morning." Frank said.

Andrew nodded. "Oh, why, oh, why, don't we get to have a normal life?"

"I thought you liked this life."

"I do."

Frank didn't bother asking.

They went to their room, and then to their bedrooms. After a few minutes, Frank fell asleep. Andrew tiptoed to his bedroom after 5 minutes and opened the door quietly.

The door squeaked.

Andrew backed away, and then he looked quietly at Frank. He was still sleeping. Andrew quietly walked over to him and softly placed a Mind Communicator on him. Andrew placed the second Mind Communicator on his head.

Andrew concentrated hard and thought, "Hey, Frank!"

Frank thought back, "Huh?"

"I'm your conscience. I just wanted to tell you that Andrew is a really awesome person."

"How come I didn't hear you before? Why are you

telling me this?"

Andrew sweated and fidgeted. Finally he got an idea. "Because you weren't ready yet!" he said.

"What made you think that? And why do you sound so much like Andrew?" Frank opened his eyes and realized who was talking to him.

"ANDREW!!!" he shouted.

Andrew rushed back to his bed and fell asleep. Frank took the Mind Communicator out of his head and snoozed.


Frank and Andrew yawned, and woke up to the sunlight peeking out from the curtains. Frank looked outside. It was sunny, and birds were chirping happily.

*It's a new day*, thought Frank.

Surprisingly, Andrew thought it was a nice day too. They rarely agreed.

When they got up and met each other, Frank said, "Come on, we need to leave this place and find Mort!"

And so they went. Andrew asked for a dollar from Frank.

Frank hesitated. "Please tell me you're not going to do anything stupid with this dollar."

"I won't." Andrew said. "And, I'm insulted."

What Andrew was thinking:

*Heh, heh, heh, he fell for it.*

Frank finally gave him one dollar. They went down to

the elevator. When they reached the first floor, Andrew walked near the clerk's desk.

WHAP!

Andrew slammed the dollar on the clerk's desk.

"Keep the change, my good man." Andrew said.

The clerk smiled, and said, "I hoped you enjoyed your stay at the Las Vegas Supersize Hotel, and come back soon!"

"Oh, we will!" said Andrew.

Frank yanked Andrew's shirt collar and they went outside.


They both looked from side to side. They walked north until they found Fremont Street. They walked along Fremont Street, and they saw a black building called D.O.O.M. In tiny letters below the banner it said:

**D**atabase **O**nline **O**perational **M**anagement.

Frank took the D.O.O.M. key out from his pocket, and they clicked the key inside the door.

"Hey, who're you?" one man asked outside, wearing a suitcase.

"My father is in there. I'm visiting him." Andrew fibbed.

"Okay, carry on."

The man walked away from them.

Andrew opened the door and went inside, and Frank closed and locked the door behind them. There was an eerie silence. Frank found the red button on the left, and he pressed it.

A huge banner unveiled saying, D.O.O.M. IS UPON YOU! The windows closed, and were covered from the inside. The ground rumbled. Alarms beeped and blared.

"Hey, what's going on?" Frank said.

"Whoa!" Andrew yelped, struggling to keep his balance on the ground.

"INTRUDER! INTRUDER!" a robotic voice yelled.

They both screamed as a white light engulfed them. The world seemed to spin, faster, and faster, until it was all a blur.

Frank and Andrew screamed, "AAAHHH!!!" in unison just before the bright light disappeared.

And they were nowhere to be found.

*Meanwhile, in Mort's lair...*

"Yes!" Mort yelled. "Now I won't have to worry about those brats anymore!"

RING! RING!

Mort's cell phone was ringing, and he picked it up.

"Hello, this is the D.O.O.M. office, which stands for **D**atabase **O**nline **O**perational **M**anagement." He said.

"What have you done with them?" a voice said.

"Excuse me?" Mort said.

*Who's this weird guy?* Mort thought.

"You know who I am."

Mort's eyes widened and his eyebrows arched upwards.

"Oh, if it isn't my old buddy, Harold Flabbergazzer! Also known as the chief of the E.S.A.F.!"

"You didn't answer my question. WHAT! HAVE! YOU! DONE! WITH! THEM?!"

Mort smirked. "Oh, those boys? I simply sent them about... 33 years back in time!"

With that, he hung up the phone.

# CHAPTER 8:
## THE TIME HOLE

"What's going on?" Frank yelled.

"I don't know!" Andrew responded.

Their bodies were twisting and stretching into different shapes. They saw pink and yellow swirling together, and they screamed. Everything became a white blur, until...

SHSHSH!

A white light came out of a hole as Frank yelled, "Whoa!" yet again and he landed on the ground. Andrew landed on top of Frank. They were in a dark alleyway.

"Ouch!" Frank yelled.

Andrew snickered.

"Where are we?" asked Frank. They got up, and dusted themselves off.

"I don't know," said Andrew promptly.

They stepped out of the alleyway and gasped. A sign said Las Vegas, Nevada. Below it said: Population: 164,674.

"It looks a little drab, don't you think?" Andrew asked. Frank nodded. He suddenly got a bad feeling in the pit of his stomach.

"I have a feeling something's wrong here." Frank said.

"Gee, you think?" Andrew asked sarcastically.

Frank shot Andrew a glare.

"What's the year, sir?" Frank asked a middle-aged man with a suitcase and hat, dressed in formal work clothes.

The man looked at Frank if he was crazy. "It's 1980! Duh!"

Frank and Andrew gasped. The man walked away, shaking his head, and muttering, "Kids these days…"

"I think Mort sent us back in time!" yelled Andrew.

Frank was doing the math. "2013… minus… 1980… equals… hmm…" he muttered.

He looked up at Andrew and said, "Mort sent us back 33 years in time!"

Andrew gasped. "What? How could he do that?"

"He didn't want us to get the gadgets, and I'm willing to bet my money that the hole that we came from is a time hole!" Frank exclaimed.

"So, how much money are you willing to bet? I've got 20 bucks in my pocket!" Andrew said, smiling mischievously.

Frank glared at Andrew.

Andrew, was now used to this. "Glares! Buy fresh Glares, made from the chef Frank himself! Only $19.99 plus $9.99 shipping and handl-" Andrew was interrupted by Frank grabbing his shirt collar.

"Shut up!" Frank hissed. "We can't get noticed. Act normal, and be serious."

"Okay, okay, serious." Andrew answered. He made a serious and sophisticated look and held it for 5 seconds before bursting out in laughter.

Frank rolled his eyes. *That's typical, coming from Andrew,* he thought.

"Well, first let's try going back into the time hole." Andrew said. They both went back inside the alleyway. No one else seemed to notice the time hole. Andrew looked down at the time hole, which was a swirling mass of pink and yellow. Suddenly, Frank pushed Andrew down into the hole.

"I'll get you for this!" Andrew yelled as he was sucked into the time hole.

Frank snickered and chuckled. He cachinnated and chortled. He chuckled and guffawed. He... well, you get the idea.

He stood back for 5 seconds, and then approached the hole. *You got what you deserved,* he thought.

SSHSHSH!

A white light was coming from the time hole.

"What's going on with the time hole?" Frank wondered out loud.

WHACK! Something kicked Frank, and he went flying to

the side. He slowly got up and saw that it was Andrew.

"Ha! Like that?" Andrew asked. "That's what you deserve."

Frank got up, and gave his brother a sulky look, which was returned by Andrew's triumphant smirk.

"How are you even here, and not in the hole?" asked Frank.

"It didn't work. Mort must have plugged up the hole." Andrew said.

"Uh oh..." said Frank.

"I can fix it," said Andrew.

"Good."

"It's going to take a while."

"Aw..."

"And it requires concentration, but I suppose I'll make do with these," Andrew said, pulling a screwdriver from his tool belt. "The time hole is connected to this outlet and power source box thingy over here." He pointed to a box on the right of the time hole. It was a box crackling with electricity with a caution sign on it.

Frank gaped at him. "Since when did you have a tool belt?"

Andrew smiled. "It's hidden so no one can see it! It's a cool gadget, just like your diary." His eyes widened at what he'd said. He scratched the back of his neck. "Um... Perhaps I've said too much."

"IT'S A JOURNAL!!!" Frank burst out. "How did you find

it?"

"Umm... Find what? I don't know what you're talking about." Andrew said.

Frank shot Andrew a glare and shook his fist at him.

"You don't know what's in store for you after this is fixed." Frank said.

Andrew fidgeted with his shirt collar. "Uh... why don't you go explore the city while I'm fixing this?" he asked.

Frank glared at Andrew again and made the **I'm-watching-you** look as he walked out of the alleyway.

*Phew,* Andrew thought. *Now, we get to work.* He unfastened the screws, attached to the time hole.

BZZTT!!

The time hole was disconnected, but not out of power yet. It was weakening.

"Level 1 of the pathetically pathetic time hole security is obliterated." Andrew said and he chuckled.

*Meanwhile, 32 years in the future...*

"GAH! They got through our Level 1 defense security system!" Mort said. "But, they won't get to Level 2 or 3!"

"Umm... I hope?"

*32 years back in time, in the old city of Las Vegas, NV...*

Frank sighed. *What is taking Andrew so long?* he thought. Frank had been strolling around the city and it felt like he had been there for hours. He decided to sit down. His legs ached.

"Finally, I got you right where I want you!" a voice said. Frank looked up. It was a man with black glasses, a black cowboy hat, and a dark red jacket.

"Do I know you?" Frank asked.

"No, but I know you! You're Andrew, right?"

"No, I'm Frank."

"Oh. I've been hired to exterminate you and your brother."

"What are you going to do?"

"Mort was very specific. He said I got to destroy you."

*Mort?* Frank thought. *Uh oh. How did I get myself into this mess?* He gulped.

The mysterious man in maroon guffawed. "Ha! You'll never come back alive!"

Frank reached for something in his pocket and stood up, then he made a horrified face.

"AAAHH! METEOR!" he screamed. The man looked back, and Frank took his laser out of his pocket and blasted the mysterious man in maroon. "Say goodbye!"

"I'll get you for this!" the man yelled as he sailed in the sky, flying left, and falling down.

THUMP.

A brown cloud of dust came from the left, made by the man.

Frank sighed. *Oops. I set it on medium power. These*

*villains never know when to stop though,* he thought.

He looked up and saw a big school. He read the name and gasped. In front of him was Hills Pine Magnet Middle School!

He walked in and looked for the 8th grade hallway.

Conveniently, there was a sign pointing to a staircase, saying:

1 flight up – 6th grade

2 flights up – 7th grade

3 flights up – 8th grade

Frank sighed. He went up the staircase, and had to stop at the second flight to catch his breath. He huffed and puffed, and continued to the 3rd flight.

At last, he was at the 8th grade floor. He nearly collapsed out of exhaustion.

It was passing time, and students were rushing through the halls.

"Excuse me," Frank asked a student, "Do you know a Harold Flabbergazzer?"

"Oh, yeah! Him!" exclaimed the student. "He just became popular because he invented a teleporter for someone. It works that if you enter coordinates..." The student's voice rambled and chattered on and on about what the teleporter could do.

*I better not do anything more here,* thought Frank. *I could change the future.*

The bell rang, and Frank walked down two flights. He

jumped and skipped down the stairs, and then he walked out of the building.

Frank quickly rushed to Andrew, who was still fixing the time portal.

"Quick, Andrew!" Frank yelled. "Did you finish fixing it?"

"Yeah, I finished!" Andrew said. "I did it extra quickly and added a new feature, where the time hole shuts down after a few seconds so someone can't get in. Maybe I added it, because you were having trouble with a mysterious man in maroon?"

Frank's mouth dropped open. "How did you…"

"Let's just say that we had an encounter. I blasted him. He doesn't look very dangerous." Andrew said.

"We've got enough on our hands now. Let's go!"

"Wait! This is a delicate process. It's rebooting. If you touch it, we'll never get back to 2013!"

"Which is why it'll be destroyed!" a voice said.

Frank and Andrew widened with shock. It was the mysterious man in maroon!

"Now that I've got you right where I wanted you…" the man said.

Frank and Andrew grimaced, backed away and prepared to get their blasters.

"I'd like to give you a free donut!"

The man handed a vanilla donut with sprinkles to Andrew.

"Bye, see you!" The man rushed away quickly.

"Well, that was strange." Andrew said. "Well, no sense in wasting perfectly good food, especially donuts!" He tried to eat the donut, but Frank stopped him.

"Wait!" Frank said. "Don't you hear a hissing sound?"

"Wait, I do!" Andrew said. Their eyes widened in realization and shock.

SSSS…

"HIT THE DECK!" Frank yelled.


They threw the donut far away from them, and hung on to the ground. The donut planted itself firmly on the ground. The ground started to rumble.

"HELP! WE'RE DOOMED!" Andrew shouted.

"SAVE US!" Frank yelled.

People screamed and cars honked as everyone was eager to get out of the exploding range. Finally, the donut exploded.

BOOM!

The sound kept repeating in Frank's ear, like a broken record. The world seemed to rattle.

The ground rumbled more. Everyone was panicking.

"Well, I guess this is the end!" Andrew said.

"I'm sorry I was mean to you!" Frank said.

"Me too!"

"Goodbye world... and 2013!"

They waited for death to come and pay them a little visit. Andrew always wondered what heaven would be like.

But, the ground stopped tremoring and they didn't hear any more explosions. Frank checked his hands. They weren't pale. He looked at the explosion. A dark black wisp of smoke was diminishing. They weren't dead!

"We're not dead!" he exclaimed.

"Hooray!" Frank and Andrew exclaimed. The boys gave each other high fives.

They checked the explosion range. If they would have moved down 2 inches, they would have been dust!

"Let's get out of here before something else happens!" Andrew said.

Their teeth were chattering and their faces were white and pale. Their eyes were wide with fear. They could still feel the heat of the explosion. Frank's legs and head ached. He just wanted to lie down and let the ground consume him.

It didn't take Einstein to figure out that they were terrified and tired from this experience. And of course, the whole "twisting their body" and "pink and yellow swirls everywhere" wouldn't really help their fear... and their stomachs. But they had to go get the gadgets back from Mort, so they prepared to jump in. Andrew set the "time hole is closed" feature to on, and they jumped in.

*A few blocks away...*

"No!" a man said, gritting his teeth. It was the mysterious man in maroon!

"They're not destroyed! Darn it, I thought the one with the blue shirt would eat it and explode. Oh, boy. Well, they better worry. I have lots of elaborate plans, and they will NOT fail this time! I am going to kill those boys, or my name isn't Dennis! Mwa ha ha!"

And then, Dennis pressed a button on his watch. He flickered and then completely disappeared.

# CHAPTER 9:
## BACK TO 2013

"Oh boy..." said Frank.

"My stomach!" groaned Andrew.

They were in the time hole. Stars danced in Andrew's eyes.

Their bodies were twisting.

*Here we go again,* thought Frank.

Surprisingly, the ceiling seemed to spit them out. They were back in the D.O.O.M. office. At last, they were back to 2013. They laid down for a minute, and then slowly got up.

"Why are we here?" asked Andrew.

"Since we got transported from here, I guess the time hole spits us out at the same place." Frank said.

"Where's Mort, anyway? I have two special surprises for him. It's called a KNUCKLE SANDWICH and for a side dish, he can taste the wrath of my laser." Andrew said, with a triumphant look.

"Oh, and by the way, don't mind what I said when we

were about to die." he said.

"Don't mind what I said either, then." Frank said.

Their eyebrows crossed at each other, and they glared at each other. Suddenly, they grinned at each other and did a fist pump.

"Well, let's find Mort!" Andrew said with another triumphant look.

"Alright, where is he, though?" Frank said.

Andrew saw a little post it note saying, "E.S.A.F. gadgets stored in Stratosphere Tower. Going to burn them in hour. Need to charge up flamethrower. 100th floor. - Mort."

"I thought the Stratosphere Tower had only 25 floors." said Frank, confused.

"Huh. Me too. Maybe you need to ask the guard for a card key or something." said Andrew, rubbing his chin.

"Well, there's no use standing here! Let's go!" Frank exclaimed.

"Alright... WAIT! Hold your horses! Stop right th-"

Andrew was interrupted by Frank yelling, "WE GET THE PICTURE!"

"Okay, geez!" Andrew rolled his eyes. "Watch me."

He took his Super-Spy glasses and carefully inspected the buttons.

"What are you doing?" Frank's eyes widened.

"Hopefully, this button is the laser..." Andrew muttered.

"Whaaat?!" Frank yelled in bewilderment.

Andrew pressed the button. He concentrated so hard that little drips of sweat began to dribble down his neck. Finally, a thin laser fired at Mort's gadgets, and they exploded. Loose remains of the gadgets were on the floor, broken.

Andrew chuckled. Frank looked at Andrew in amazement, and said, "You, sir, are a loose cannon."

"Why thank you, kind sir." Andrew blew the smoke off his glasses. "I try."

Andrew wiped the sweat off his neck.

"Hey, get your sweat away from me!" Frank said. "I didn't know you had to concentrate to fire a laser."

"It seemed like the right thing to do," Andrew said. "Now that we're done horsing around, let's go to the Stratosphere Tower. What's the address?"

"I don't know. Let me look it up." Frank said. Mort's laptop remained safe, and it was on. Frank walked over to it, and looked at it. He gritted his teeth. The screen read: Mort, evil genius. Enter password:

"Great, it's locked." Frank said with an angry expression.

"Let me try!" Andrew exclaimed.

"Okay, but I don't think -" Frank was interrupted by a logging in sound. His mouth gaped open. "How did you -"

"I just tried the password, 'E.S.A.F. stinks,' and it worked."

They both cracked up. Frank looked up the address on Google. It read:

2000 South Las Vegas Boulevard

Las Vegas, NV 89104

(702) 380-7777

"Cool!" Andrew exclaimed.

"Alright, we'll get into a taxi." Frank said. "Let's get out of here!" Frank closed the page, and locked Mort's laptop.

They walked out of the D.O.O.M. office. Luckily, Frank still had the key, so he locked the door.

Andrew whistled. They waited for a taxi to come. 5 minutes passed and nothing came. So they went back in the D.O.O.M. office and unlocked the laptop again. Frank looked up the number for the taxi service. There was a website called, "Las Vegas Taxi Cabs | Get a ride! 702-888-4888 | HOME"

They called the number using Mort's cell phone. Frank spoke.

"Hello? We'd like a taxi to come. Place? Um, the Database Online Operational Management office. 250 Fremont Street. Okay, we'll wait. Alright, bye." Frank hung up.

"Okay, let's wait outside. The ride should be here in a few minutes." he said.

"Sure!" Andrew said.

They walked outside whistling. Frank locked the door, as usual. They waited until the taxi came. It would take 5 minutes, so they sat down near the doors of the D.O.O.M. headquarters, and waited.

Finally, the taxi came. They got inside and Andrew said, "To Stratosphere Tower, please."

"Address?" the taxi man grunted.

Andrew whispered to Frank, "Looks like someone got up on the wrong side on the bed today."

"Address??" the taxi man grumbled again, this time louder.

"Um... what was it... Oh yeah! 2000 South Las Vegas Boulevard!"

The taxi man sighed and drove to the required address. It was a short ride.

Andrew relaxed and laid down. "It feels good to be in a taxi, without blowing up villains and other etcetera."

"You said it." Frank answered. He also began to relax. And then, the taxi stopped.

"So soon? That was like a 5 minute ride!" Andrew complained.

"That's five dollars." the taxi man said, with an expression of distaste which also said: I don't get paid enough to do this.

Frank got a $10 bill to the taxi man. The taxi man gave him five dollars back for change. Frank and Andrew got out of the taxi, and the taxi sped away.

"Well, he was definitely grumpy." said Frank.

"Why don't they give us a little respect?" asked Andrew, inquiring. "They don't even know we're the legendary Andrew and Frank."

"It's FRANK and Andrew."

"What-EVER!" Andrew rolled his eyes.

Frank gave Andrew a deadpan expression. "Alright, let's do this."

# CHAPTER 10:
## 100<sup>TH</sup> FLOOR?

They burst into the building. No one noticed them except the security guy.

"Who are you people?" the security man asked.

"I'm Frank, and this is Andrew!" Frank replied.

"We're going to inspect the elevator for a minute."

"Fine." the security man said. He went back to reading a cheesy romance novel called, **As the Tide Turns**.

Frank and Andrew walked over to the elevator. Frank pushed the up button. The elevator came down, so they stepped in. The doors closed. Frank and Andrew searched for a 100 button, but they could not find it anywhere, so Andrew pressed the open door button. The door opened, and Frank and Andrew walked to the security guy.

"Hey!" Andrew yelled.

The security man nearly jumped. "What do you want?" he said.

"Where's the 100<sup>th</sup> floor?" asked Frank.

*Is it me, or did the security man's eyebrows cross?* Frank thought.

"100th floor? There are only 25 floors in the Stratosphere tower! Do your homework." the security man said.

"Come on, we know there's a 100th floor." replied Andrew.

"THERE IS NO 100th FLOOR!" yelled the security guy.

Everyone stared at the security man. He nervously chuckled and said sheepishly, "Carry on."

Everyone got back to doing whatever they were doing.

"Come on! TELL ME HOW TO GET THERE! I need to defeat a villain! I could blast you with my laser!" yelled Frank.

The security man's eyes bulged and he turned pale. He gave Frank a key. "Make sure no one is in the elevator with you." he whispered.

"About time..." Andrew muttered.

The security man went back to reading the novel he was attached to.

Frank and Andrew walked over to the elevator and pressed the down button. The elevator instantly opened. They walked in, and Andrew clicked the close door button. Frank saw a last glimpse of the security guy frowning at them, before the doors closed.

Andrew inserted the key inside the key slot. Astronaut suits came out, and Frank and Andrew put them on. A new button also popped out, saying 100. Frank pressed it. The button glowed orange. For a minute, nothing happened. Then, the elevator shot up so fast, it felt like they were traveling at the speed of light!

"Whoa!!" Frank yelled.

"Not.... cool!!" Andrew grimaced, his eyes wide.

Then 5 seconds later, the door opened, and Frank and Andrew collapsed, breathing heavily. They slowly got to their feet, removed the suits, and walked out. The elevator doors closed behind them, and it shot down at speeds that would have caused a human to pop if they weren't wearing the astronaut suit. They looked down. They were at the top of a mountain, and below them was the Stratosphere Tower. Andrew turned pale, even though there were barriers to protect people from falling. Frank noticed Andrew's reaction, and he pulled Andrew away.

"Are you okay?" asked Frank.

Andrew nodded slowly. "Sorry, but you know that..."

"Yeah, I know about your acrophobia." Frank said.

Andrew's face was glum, and he looked down at his toes.

"Well, all we have to do is walk across this...scary...rickety...old... bridge... oh, dear..." Frank said.

"Okay!" Andrew said. "You've scared me enough!"

And so, they walked to the bridge while Andrew nervously fidgeted with his shirt collar.

"Okay, just hold on the straps of the bridge and DO. NOT. LOOK. DOWN." Frank ordered. "I'll be right behind you."

Andrew simply nodded, and they went on the bridge.

He couldn't help but think, *One false step, and I could*

*fall to my doom.*

He put that thought away for a minute and replaced it with a reassuring thought that said, *You can do this, Andrew. Just look straight ahead. Don't look down.*

Before they knew it, they had crossed the bridge. Andrew grinned while Frank patted Andrew on the shoulder.

They looked out and saw a large building that said, "Mort's lair."

Andrew grinned devilishly. "Let's do this."

Frank and Andrew said "One! Two! Three!!" in unison and they broke down the door.

CRASH!

Mort's door burst open. It was not put together very well. Frank and Andrew were expecting something like lasers or a brick wall. Mort looked up at the two boys, clearly uninterested.

"What do you want?" asked Mort, yawning.

Something about Mort's attitude irritated Frank. He resisted the urge to blast Mort.

Andrew, on the other hand, didn't resist. He shot a laser at Mort. He ducked, and it hit an E.S.A.F. gadget.

Frank frowned at Andrew. Andrew's eyebrows furrowed. "Oops."

"Listen, buddy, give us back the gadgets, NOW." Frank said.

"Why should I? What can two kids do?" Mort said.

"Hey! I didn't go back in time to escape some man in maroon, survive an exploding donut, and nearly dying, for you to tell me that you're NOT going to give us BACK the gadgets!" Frank yelled furiously. He seemed to be blowing with rage.

Mort's eyes widened when Frank said, "escape some man in maroon."

*Did Dennis really fail?* Mort thought.

"Surrender now!" Frank yelled.

"Never!" Mort said.

"Don't say I didn't warn you. It's two against one!"

"Oh, really?"

Mort pressed a button on his watch. For a moment, nothing happened.

Andrew laughed out loud. "What's that supposed to do?"

CRASH!

# CHAPTER 11:
## DEFEATING MORT

A man burst through the ceiling. It was Dennis, with a jetpack on his back! Bits of plaster rained on Frank, Andrew, and Mort's heads.

"Did I miss out on the fun?" Dennis asked, grinning evilly.

Frank grimaced. *Did the villains never stop?*

Mort smirked at Frank and Andrew. "Nope, you're just in time for me to annihilate them."

Dennis lowered himself on the ground, and he threw his jetpack aside on the table.

"Now the odds are a bit more even, don't you think?" asked Mort, grinning.

"No." said Andrew.

"Quiet!" Mort snapped. "Now we will defeat you once and for all!"

"I think it's the other way around!" exclaimed Andrew.

"That's enough! We gave you a chance, and you refused, so that means, BRING IT ON!" Frank yelled as he charged.

Andrew groaned and shook his head. *He always overreacts.*

And then, he also charged.

It was safe to safe that it was a foolish decision.

Lasers were everywhere, (courtesy of Mort), and Frank and Andrew were dodging them like crazy!

"Whoa!" Andrew yelled. "Help!"

He kept running backwards, and backwards, trying to avoid the lasers.

"Whoa!" he yelled yet again, and he dodged another laser, which nearly sliced his ear off! Snippets of hair fell from his head. He glared angrily at Mort. "Frank!"

For a split second, Frank's eyes locked with Andrew's. They both were thinking the same thing, which didn't happen very often. *The best defense is a good offense.*

Now, Frank and Andrew went on the offensive. They shot lasers at Mort and he was the one that was dodging now. Frank and Andrew snickered and momentarily forgot about Dennis.

Dennis was behind a cannon, charging a blast quietly. The blast was really slow, but if it hit you, it could ruin your day. It was the most powerful laser in all history of lasers. So when Frank and Andrew were distracted fighting Mort, Dennis fired the blast.

BAM! It shot towards Frank and Andrew.

"Yikes!" Frank said. He got out the way, but Andrew didn't. He stood frozen in fear, staring at the humongous red laser coming towards him. Frank shook his head, and dashed to Andrew. Frank pulled Andrew's shirt collar, and pushed him out of the way.

"Whoa!" Mort yelled. The blast was coming right at him!

The blast slammed into him, and he screamed. The laser blew a hole in the wall, and it kept going straight while Mort fell to his doom. "HELP!"

THUMP.

A small white cloud of dust emerged from the bottom of the pit.

Dennis cringed. There was a moment of silence, and then Frank and Andrew burst into cheers.

"We finally defeated Mort!" Andrew said.

"Nooo!! Our plan is ruined!" Dennis yelled.

Frank and Andrew stared at him. Dennis cowered in fear.

Frank and Andrew rolled their eyes and set their laser to high power. Then they blasted Dennis, together. It made another hole in the wall while Dennis fell to his doom. "Noooo-ooo!"

THUMP.

Another small white cloud of dust emerged from the pit.

There was another moment of silence, and Frank spoke up:

"You know, they were really evil. But I didn't want them to DIE."

"Yeah, but what's done is done, even though we feel bad." Andrew said.

"Okay, let's bring the gadgets back to the E.S.A.F. Now, how do we do that?"

Andrew looked around, and picked up a nearby gadget.

"Hey, look! It's the Teleportalight 5000!" Frank said.

"Uh, cool. How do you work this thing?" Andrew questioned.

Andrew typed in the coordinates: 58.5°N, 154°W. He clicked the TRANSPORT button.

"Hey! Wait!" Frank yelled.

The room glowed with an intensive bright yellow light, then Frank, Andrew, and the gadgets disappeared.

FLASH!

Frank, Andrew and the gadgets were floating 2 feet above land. They dropped down into... snow? A raging snowstorm was starting.

"Great job, GENIUS, you dropped us into the barren tundra!" Frank yelled at Andrew.

"Well, SORRY, but I don't know the coordinates!" Andrew yelled back.

"Give me that gadget!" Frank grabbed the Teleportalight 5000 from Andrew and clicked on the map. Frank punched in the address of the E.S.A.F. and the map showed these coordinates: 36°N, 115°W. The screen said, "Okay? Press Transport button." Frank looked around and clicked the TRANSPORT button.

The tundra glowed with yellow light reflected by the wet snow. Then the light disappeared.

FLASH!

*Meanwhile, in the chief's office...*

"I hope those boys are okay," the chief said, sorting out papers. "If Mort gets a hold of them, there's no telling what he'd do! He could use them for ransom, or..." The chief's voice trailed off.

He shook his head. "What am I saying? They'll get back the gadgets. But it'll take hard work. I mean, it's not like they'll just flash into this room carrying all the gadgets."

He chuckled, thinking about how funny he was, and suddenly...

FLASH!

Frank, Andrew and the gadgets were floating in midair. The chief's eyes widened.

"Whoa!" Frank said as they dropped. CRASH!

They fell on the table.

The chief, however, wasn't so lucky. All the gadgets fell on his head!

"Mom! It's raining rocks?!" he said, and then fainted.

Frank and Andrew, took a look at the chief, and said, "Uh oh."

*One minute later...*

"One, two, three!" Frank and Andrew both counted.

Then, they dumped the ice cold water on the chief.

"Ack! Who? What? When? Where? Why?!" the chief screamed.

"Oh, it's just you two." The chief glared at the two boys. He was sopping wet, and dried himself with a towel, and the InstaDry 2000. He shook his head. Water sprayed everywhere.

"Hey!" Frank yelled. Finally, the chief was dry.

A moment of silence passed before the chief asked, "So was your mission successful? You defeated Mort?"

Frank and Andrew nodded. "He fell off a ledge."

The chief's face darkened. He appeared to be thinking about something.

"Okay, then, you boys relax and go back home while I clean up this mess."

Frank and Andrew grinned. "Okay, chief! Whenever you need help, call us!"

They rushed to the elevator and stepped in. Loud heavy metal music screamed in their ears.

"AAAAHHH!!!" Andrew screamed, holding his ears.

*Here we go again,* thought Frank.

They exited the elevator, went outside, and locked the door.

"Ah, back to the old city." Frank said. Cars were beeping their horns everywhere. There was so much traffic that the cars only seemed to be moving an inch per minute. There was lots of car exhaust in the air. They listened to the noise.

BEEP! BEEP!

"Hey, move forward!"

"Shut up!"

"Hey, I've got a talent show to go to!"

"Why can't you all just move?!"

"Who's holding up the line? I demand he or she will hear from my lawyer!"

Frank and Andrew shook their heads.

"Oh, yeah. This isn't the old city. It's the new city. We visited the old city 32 years ago." Andrew said.

Frank was about to glare at Andrew, but he just shook his head, and said, "All's well that ends well, right, Andrew?"

"Yeah, yeah, whatever." Andrew replied. "Want to go to the Supersize hotel and relax?"

"Oh, well, it couldn't hurt!"

And so they went, running off in the distance to the hotel, together.

# ABOUT THE AUTHOR

Pranav Mahesh is currently a sixth grader who lives in Fairfield, CT. He loves to write and play with his brother, and his favorite subjects are math, and reading. Watch for the next book in The Adventures of Frank and Andrew series, coming soon!

Printed in Great Britain
by Amazon.co.uk, Ltd.,
Marston Gate.